Symphony of My Heart

Shervin Hojat, PhD

Symphony of My Heart

Shervin Hojat, PhD

www.shervinhojat.com

Tiber Pubs, LLC

Austin, Texas

www.tiberpubs.com

Copyright © 2018 Shervin Hojat, 2018

First Published in the United States of America

ISBN: 978-0-9818969-5-3

Cover image by: Shutterstock 610965833

Cover designed by: Zora Alexandra Knauf

To those whose hearts are broken open with love

To those who have lost their minds

To those who dared to be vulnerable

To those who are seeking bliss

To those who choose to live fully

To those who have dreams

To those who feel lucky

To those who have a deep longing

Table of Contents

Invitation 1

Anticipation 13

The Lover 19

My Love 33

Our Union 49

Separation 67

Longing 79

Pleading 93

Reflections 105

Acknowledgments... 117

About the Author 119

Invitation

I may not know what I want to do;

I do know what I want to be.

I want to be the sun magnifying your beauty.

I want to be the moon lighting your path.

I want to be the wind that caresses your neck.

I want to be the air flowing into your lungs.

I want to be the eye shadow lining your eyes.

I want to be the decoration tied in your hair.

I want to be the lemon in your water.

I want to be the strawberry crushed by your mouth.

I want to be the pillow that allows you to rest.

I want to be the sheet that engulfs you.

Let me hear your voice;

Let me hear your giggles.

Let me see your pearly teeth;

Let me see your shining lips.

Let me watch your dance;

Let me watch your seductive gestures.

Let me feel the joy of my sunrise;

Let me feel the love of God.

When moon looks at sun,

Moon only sees radiant love.

Moon does not see the surface blemishes;

Moon sees and feels much deeper.

Consume me, my darling.

Consume me with your mesmerizing eyes.

Consume me with your love and passion.

Consume me with your elegance and beauty.

Consume me with your tender touch.

Be yourself.

Shine your loving rays, my darling;

You are perfect the way you are.

When you hear your lover's voice,

Let go of who said what and rejoice.

Let go of who did what and rejoice.

Listen to your inner voice;

Experience your beloved with a choice.

Ignore the spoken or unspoken words.

Let us become one again.

Let us be a source of joy and laughter.

Let us be an example of faith and trust.

Let us abandon what weakens us.

Let our love make us invincible.

Let our love make us childlike.

Let our love give us the wings to fly together.

Cannot disguise my love for you

Cannot suppress my heart's purple hue

Cannot hide what is true

My eyes give me away

My joy at hearing your voice gives me away

My excitement at seeing you gives me away

Kiss me with your lips.

Kiss me with your song.

Kiss me with your eyes.

Kiss me with your heart.

Look into my eyes;

Hear my unspoken words.

Look into my eyes;

Hear my unsung melodies.

Touch my tears gently.

Each teardrop is a page,

Crafted in the sanctuary of my heart.

Brush my face gently;

Remind me it is OK to let go.

Caress my hands softly;

Remind me I am not alone.

Hold me warmly;

Remind me I am home again.

Anticipation

The bird flying out of the cage
To his love in the bright open sky—

Sense of anticipation
Sense of elation
Sense of desire and aim
Sense of merging with the flame

The bird reaching the majestic sun

Deep, dark depression

No desire to do anything.

In a flash, the darkness

Is turned into brightness and excitement.

What changed?

A thought!

A vision that tomorrow is time for reunion.

Tomorrow is time for letting go of old hurts.

Tomorrow is time to feel God's love and joy again.

I opened my eyes

I looked for you

I did not find you

It was all dark and dull

I closed my eyes

I found you in my heart's eyes

My world grew light and vibrant

I welcomed my sunrise

Oh, my love,

I feel your presence deep inside my chest.

You bring me joy—

The joy

Of hearing your voice

Of holding you tight

Of reunion

Of becoming complete

The joy of living in bliss.

The Lover

Learn love from the lovers.

Ocean and shoreline are lovers.

No matter how many times they see each other,

They rush toward each other

As if it were their first encounter.

I am everything one day;

I am nothing the next.

I am invincible one day;

I am broken the next.

I am full of joy and hope one day;

I am depressed and sad the next.

What makes the days different?

It is the presence of my lover!

It is the end to our separation.

I am the leaf;

You are the branch.

I am the petals;

You are the rose bush.

I am the smile;

You are the joy.

I am the misty rain;

You are the cloud.

I am the warmth;

You are the sun.

I am the lover;

You are the love.

Your face in my mind,

Your voice whispering in my ear,

Your hands sparking sensation on my body,

Your breath blowing fire on my neck,

Your love stirring joy in my heart—

This is what keeps me alive.

My dear love,

You are in my breath,
You are in my heart,
You are in my thoughts.

You and I are one,
Breathing together under the glorious sun.

I am a slave.

I am a slave to my love.

The chain of slavery is my deep love for you;

It pulls me wherever you go.

Where would I want to be if I had only five years to live?

The answer is with my love.

Where would I want to be if I had only a year to live?

The answer is with my love.

Where would I want to be if I had only one month to live?

The answer is with my love.

Time is running out!

Why you do not run to your love?

Why you do not listen to your heart?

Will I live a life that is expected of me?

Or

Will I live a life that excites me?

Will I live a life bereft of love?

Or

Will I embrace my love?

I have simple desires:

To be with my love

To become fully alive

To experience oneness

To experience Heaven on Earth

Why now?

Why this way?

Do not question it, my love;

Drink from the cup of joy and laughter.

Without you, my life is empty.

Without you, my life is only memories.

Without you, my life is a body without a heart.

Without you, my life is a bird without a song.

Without you, my life is a thousand years without sunshine.

Without you, my life is a rose bush without any roses.

Without you, my life is a dance without any music.

My Love

You are the rain
In the hot desert.

You are the cool wind
In the summer night.

You are the bright star
In the dark, lonely night.

You are the water
For the thirsty flowers.

You are the relief
For the aching heart.

You are the food
For the hungry soul.

You are the missing piece
To the puzzle of my life.

Your eyes are a resting place for the lost,

A light in the dark of night,

A safe haven for the wounded,

A reminder of universal love,

An incubator of smiles.

Your eyes are a remedy for my ailment.

I have lost a part of me!

Walking with a hole in my soul,
Walking with a feeling of intense incompleteness,
My beloved has taken my heart.

Next to my love,

It is the best of times.

Far away from my love,

It is the worst of times.

I worship the God who created you.

I kiss the hands of the mother who birthed you.

I praise the angels who kept you innocent.

I adore the ground you walk on.

I savor the air that comes through your lungs.

I cherish you every moment of my existence.

My love,

My love for you is like an ever-growing plant.

It grows by the second and the minute.

It grows as you shine your love on my heart.

It grows as I know you better.

It grows as I know me better.

It grows as we laugh together.

It grows as we cry together.

It grows as we protect one another.

It grows as we talk about our divine dreams.

It grows as we feel gratitude in our hearts.

My lover is like an ocean—

Calm, beautiful, intriguing, nurturing,

Unpredictable, fiery, playful, and mysterious.

I am in love with you, my love,

As the ocean is in love with the shoreline.

No matter how many times you push me away,

I come back each day to embrace you and stay.

Your eyes are like the most magnificent tree,
Beautiful, mesmerizing, breathtaking.

Your eyes are fed by pristine waters,
Rooted inside the strongest mountains,
Surrounded by brightly colored flowers,
Nest for a myriad of colorful birds.

Your eyes are a universe within a universe,
Giving the sun and the moon a reason to rise,
Playing life's orchestra of love and joy.

You give me life

You take away my breath

You are the joy in my garden of love

With you, my life is content.

With you, my smiles and laughter come often.

With you, my discomforts are forgotten.

With you, my body is vibrant.

With you, my fears are silent.

With you, my life is a treat.

With you, my life is complete.

Without you, my life is torment.

The hummingbird joyfully feeds on the nectar of the flower.

The butterfly transforms itself to fly to the flower.

The bee bathes itself in the pollen of the flower.

You are my beginning and end.

You are the pollen that brings new life to me.

You are the nutrients that my soul craves.

You are my nectar.

You are my joy.

You are my destination.

The sun awakens to admire you.

The moon rises to admire you.

The clouds gather to admire you.

My love, there is nothing better than

Admiring your beauty and elegance.

Oh, my love,

Your voice awakens me,

Your voice reminds me,

There is still something more to long for.

Our Union

Your eyes,

Envoys from the mystical universe

Your eyes,

Bright stars in dark of night

Your eyes,

Universe within a universe

Your eyes,

Ambassadors of your love

Hold on tight to your mesmerizing beloved.

Hold on tight to your one of a kind.

Hold her tight with all your might;

Let her light brighten your dark night.

She is your soul's delight;

She is the gift to the knight.

My love is like an ocean.

Whenever she touches me, I become calm and pure.

A gift, not hidden in wrappings,

A gift, not intended to impress others,

A gift, not intended to show status and wealth,

A gift, simple, unwrapped, yet priceless.

A glance into your eyes, deep,

With many meanings,

No need for spoken words.

In the heat of a summer night,

Hot winds ravage her face and body.

Dark-brown eyes aglow with light,

Breathing in the passionate, hot air.

Her body grows warmer and firmer,

An enticing smile showing off her delight.

The thirsty lover comes closer to heaven's gate,

Drowning her lover in tears of joy.

He seeks the heavenly nectar,

To quash his eternal thirst.

Drinking honey and cherry juice,

From the fountain of eternal love.

A gift so precious

A memory so innocent and fresh

A connection so familiar and everlasting

A love so pure

An event celebrated in the heavens

Oneness of our hearts

Oneness of our souls

Your shining lips

Are the light in the darkness of eclipse.

Your succulent lips

Are an invitation to my own.

At dawn

You woke me with your tender touch.

You woke me with your fragrant smell.

You woke me with your soft lips.

You were inside my head.

You were on my body.

A free flow of energy,

like two rivers merging at last in the ocean.

No expectations.

Just a profound longing to share

Our divine love

With one another.

On the darkest of nights,

You are the ever-burning candle.

On the coldest of nights,

You are the constant warmth.

In the midst of overwhelming hate,

You are the reminder of love.

In the most troubling moments of self-doubt,

You are magically comforting.

The moon shining in the dark night

The red and white rose petals lying on the stairs

The exotic flowers by the tub

Their fragrance making lovers drunk

She with glowing cherry lips

Ripe for everlasting sips

No touch is like your touch.

No love is like your love.

No gaze is like your gaze.

No kiss is like your kiss.

No day is as fun,

No meal as delicious,

Without you.

Your lips are shiny and inviting,

Open and welcoming,

Proud and elegant,

Delicious as a ripe strawberry.

Your lips are the holder of many desires,

An eternal well of nectar,

The cup from which I drink the nectar of your love.

Your lips are the igniter of eternal fire,

Burning me,

I rise like the Phoenix.

Bring your lips closer to my lips

So I may gaze into your eyes,

Fascinated by your beauty and grace of soul.

Bring your lips closer to my lips

So I may smell the fragrance of your hair,

Hearing the rapid pounding of your heart.

Bring your lips closer to my lips

So I may breathe in the passion of your breath,

Tasting the sweetness of your mouth.

When I am with you, my love,

You bring out the best in me.

My breath is joyful;

My steps have strength.

My life has purpose;

I feel alive.

When I am away from you,

I do not like who I become.

My soul diminishes;

I feel immense emptiness.

My life becomes meaningless;

I feel lost and disoriented.

Separation

Waking up at dawn,

I search for my love.

I find no trace

Except for:

Her warmth in my heart and mind,

Her scent in my nose,

Her laughter in my ears.

Come to me, my love.

A deep longing,

Within the corners of my soul:

To be with you

To gaze into your eyes

To hold you

To love you forever and ever.

Imprisoned by my body and circumstances,

With many unspoken words stuck in my throat,

I awake filled with deep desire and longing.

I cried tonight.

It was the cry of being alive,

Of being loved,

Of overwhelming love in my heart.

It was the cry of being apart.

I miss you very much, my love;
Separation is no longer bearable.

Without you my life is empty;
With you I am alive.

My love,
I want to be alive forever.

Our long separation has made us vigilant.

Our long separation has made us impatient.

Yet our love has made us persistent.

Cannot take sunshine away from a rose,

Cannot take stars away from the night,

Cannot take water away from a fish,

Cannot take air away from a bird.

My love is a skilled hunter;
She loves the rush of the quest.

My love is a skilled hunter;
She hunts with her words and smiles.

My love is a skilled hunter;
She hunts with her mind and beauty.

My love is a skilled hunter;
She hunts with her sorrow and tears.

My love is a skilled hunter;
She pierces hearts in the dark of night.

On the ground, weak in the net of my love,
Begging for mercy and compassion,
"Devour me now!"

It hurts too much when you abandon me
And go hunting for other prey.

The day I became alive:

When you lovingly gazed into my eyes

And told me that I make you happy.

The day I died:

When you looked at me with anger and

Said that you are happier without me.

I am part of you,

no matter how far you run away.

I am part of you,

no matter how much you deny me.

I bring you joy,

no matter how much you pretend otherwise.

I will be there

when you return.

You said you would be by my side.

You left when I needed you most.

Longing

As my feet touch the soft sands,
My hands search for yours.

As the wind caresses my face,
I search for your soft, inviting lips.

As the sun warms my body,
I search for you to warm my heart.

As the waves run steadily toward the shore,
I search for you on the horizon.

As I watch couples make footprints in the sand,
I sigh and implore you to walk our walk.

My heart is sad;
I feel an intense longing.

The longing to hear your voice,
The longing to laugh with you,
The longing to feel you near me.

I know we promised to be patient.
I am impatiently patient!

Sleep, my angel.
I am waiting for you.

My love has not spoken,

Yet I can hear the unspoken.

It adds fuel to my internal fire,

This yearning for my love.

Profound longing to end this trial of separation

Profound longing to hold each other and

Erase the pain of separation

Profound longing to celebrate and rejoice again

What do I desire?

To see you again,

To experience the light in your eyes,

To bask in your smile,

To hear your giggles,

To dream with you,

To walk with you,

To eat with you,

To cry and laugh with you,

To adore you,

To remember Heaven on Earth.

The intense longing for reunion

The excitement for communion

My deepest desire is to be by you

To have my dream come true

To become whole again

To become sane again

Oh, my love,

I feel your presence deep inside my chest;

You bring me tremendous joy.

The joy of hearing your voice,

The joy of holding you tight,

The joy of reunion,

The joy of becoming complete,

The joy of living in bliss.

My love, I desire to
Share the melody of my heart.

My love, I desire to
Hold your beautiful, soft hands.

My love, I desire to
Look into your pristine eyes.

My love, I desire to
Hold you tight until we melt into one.

My love, I desire to
Show the world your beauty and power.

My love, I desire to
Have you physically near me.

Sense of freedom,
Sense of calmness,
Sense of ease.

Hope is my last mantra:

Hope that tomorrow will be different,

Hope that my love calls me,

Hope that she keeps her promise.

Oh, majestic ocean, wash away my grief.

Oh, pristine waters, purify my heart.

Oh, powerful tides, take away what no longer serves me.

Oh, refreshing breeze, take me home to my love.

At dusk, I searched for my love
In the empty room.

At lunch, I searched for my love
In vacant seats.

At the beach, I searched for my love
On desolate shores.

At the dance, I searched for my love
Among many strangers.

Where are you, my love?
Bring your heart near me.
Bring your lips near mine.

The time is now!
Come, come, my love.

Pleading

My love,

My beautiful angel,

Do not lose your hope;

Do not lose your will.

You may feel hopeless.

You may feel disappointed in others,

Yet you are not powerless.

Smile despite your temporary challenges.

Be a bright light in the dark night.

There are paths, yet unknown to you,

For fulfilling your wish.

Expect miracles.

Let go of what you cannot control;

Remember who you are.

My love,

You are special.

You are not alone.

I adore you.

Oh, Creator of all that is,

There is no pain greater than

Seeing pain in the eyes of my beloved.

Oh, Creator of all that is,

Erase the pain from my love.

Bring back the sparkle in her eyes.

My love has many lovers.

I am at the mercy of my beloved's lovers.

They are selfish;

They try to keep me separated from my lover.

Oh, lovers, you know the pain of separation.

Do not do what is painful to other lovers.

Let me, my love.

Let me wake you with my kisses.

Let me wake you with my touches.

Let me wake you with my smiles.

Let me wake you with my joyful eyes.

Let me wake you with my love.

Let me.

God has a cruel sense of humor.

He puts love in the hearts of lovers;
Then he separates them.

He enjoys seeing lovers suffer;
He enjoys seeing lovers cry.

He enjoys seeing lovers feel incomplete.

God is a great teacher to lovers.

He pairs lovers with their opposites.

He teaches them lessons about choice.

He teaches them lessons about patience.

He teaches them lessons about courage.

He teaches lessons about destiny.

He teaches them lessons about moments.

My flower,
Open up.

Do not allow the sorrow of separation wilt you;
Thrive.

Show your face;
Blossom.

Show your beauty;
Radiate.

It does not matter

how long youth and beauty last.

It does not matter

how long this experience will last.

It does not matter

what happened before, or

what will happen in the future.

It does not matter.

Be the expression of who you are now!

Stay by me

Give me your attention

Listen to the melody of my heart

Feel the vibration of my soul

Reflections

When you fall in love with someone

Who does not love herself,

No matter how much she loves you,

She will hurt you by not loving herself.

Follow your heart!

If you follow your heart,
Your soul will feel alive.

If you follow your heart,
Your body will feel light.

If you do not follow your heart wholly,
You will kill your soul slowly.

If you do not follow your heart.
You will be dead from the start.

If you do not follow your heart with play,
You will be a lifeless butterfly in a display.

I once was grounded in reason;

I could overcome emotions by rationalization

I am now a slave to my heart;

It resists the tyranny of my mind.

Logic's fear of future has lost its pull;

Logic's appeal to be strong does not distract me.

Your love now resides in my heart;

I now resist the tyranny of an empty heart.

Logic and reason were kings for five decades;
They have now lost their starring roles.

The new king is my longing heart.
The new king is my thirsty heart,

Looking for love and reunion.
Logic and reason are now my servants.

In the presence of love,

The old grow young.

In the presence of love,

Logic runs away.

In the presence of love,

Every thought is of reunion.

Love does not kill;
Love brings life.

Do not ask about love
From those with no experience.

Look in the eye of a lover,
And you will know the real story.

Look at the face of the lover meeting her lover;
The sparkle of love is manifest.

It is said you become crazy when you fall in love.

Yes, love makes you distracted.

Yes, love makes you irrational.

Yes, love makes you impatient.

You are even crazier if you do not experience love.

Love is a gift from God.

Get crazy, irrational, and impatient for sake of love!

Tears and longing are only understood by
those whose hearts have been broken by love.

I don't fear death;

I die every day without you.

I don't fear living;

I have tasted life with you.

I can die today, or

I can live today.

Acknowledgments

Special thanks to Zora Alexandra Knauf, who designed the book cover and beautifully laid out the book. Zora made me feel very supported in the process.

I'd like to thank Judi Heidel, who edited my poetry and made my poems flow with ease without losing the soul of the writing.

I'd like to thank my dear friend Amy Gillespie, who encouraged me during the life of the book and introduced me to Zora.

I am also grateful to Laurie Rivers, who was an inspiration and a great source of encouragement.

About the Author

Shervin Hojat, is the author of *Tend To Your Garden Within*, 2009, the product of many years of refining and seeking his spirituality and his life's purpose.

Shervin has a PHD in Electrical Engineering and he works as a software engineer in a high-tech company in San Diego, CA. He takes time each day to pause, reflect, and connect to nature and its inhabitants. When not out exploring and photographing his friends in nature, Shervin spends his time in meditation, self-reflection, contemplating the dynamics of relationships, and inspiring others to realize their potential through his writing and programs.

For book readings and sales please contact Shervin Hojat at shervin@shervinhojat.com. You can visit his website at www.shervinhojat.com.